Foreword

When I first ventured into the real estate industry years ago, I did so with the goal of helping people find their dream home. In my years of experience, not only have I helped numerous clients, but I've also accumulated years of knowledge to help them more effectively.

I decided to share all of my expertise in one place with potential clients in my Selling Secrets book and now I am sharing that expertise with other agents. I want to help you have the best possible career in real estate. Being a real estate agent in today's world is more than passing a test and finding a broker to host your license. It requires dedication and a team of support to guide you. When you have the support you need and the tools necessary to stand out from the rest of the thousands of agents out there, meeting your goals of becoming a successful agent becomes much easier.

This book contains insider advice on the home-selling process, tips and tricks to help you achieve your ultimate real estate goals.

If you want to become part of a progressive, growing, state of the art group of agents that is expanding across the world, my doors are open to help you get started! Whether you are an experienced agent or just getting started, nothing is more important than being connected to a company and a group that is supportive, and forward thinking.

I am thrilled to be able to offer you this book and share some of the experience I have gained through the years. My hope is that you will take away something that will help you gain momentum and become the success you envision for your real estate career.

About Janna Valencia

I was raised in Palestine, TX with 3 siblings. As a child, I had aspirations of being a veterinarian. Never, in a million years, did I think I would go into the real estate industry, but you can't always predict where or when you will discover what you are meant to do in life.

I was taught at a young age that if you want something in life, you have to work for it. That is what I did...I worked hard. Later, I learned there is more to it than just working hard but it helped me gain a lot of skill in working effectively to get the most of the effort I was putting in.

As the years went by, I worked my way to management in the retail world and eventually started my own business, always resolved to be the best version of myself.

I first got into the real estate industry in 1996, convinced by my mother, also a long time successful real estate agent. I had a bad experience in the first year of my career as an agent and I got out of the industry for a while. I went on to own my own business and after selling it I got my real estate license again. That was the beginning of the journey that is providing me with much joy and with every transaction adding to my family of happy people who can enjoy their lives a little better.

In this stage of my career, I am surrounding myself with like minded people who are independent, hard working people who are also making a difference in the lives of the families they serve. I am a firm believer in communication and consider myself great at building relationships.

I pride myself in treating each client and team member as a member of my family, conducting the business with them as if it were my own transaction. I think it is important to put yourself in their shoes, to an extent, to serve them better.

I live in San Antonio, TX with her 2 Yorkies, Kassidy and Kobe. I love San Antonio's family atmosphere and the charm of its history. In my free time, I enjoy writing books and taking adventures to the country, exploring the history and architecture of old structures and the charm of small towns. I also like to visit the lakes nearby, if only to sit and listen to the water lapping the shore. I am also a Mexico traveler. I am enamored with the beauty and culture of the country. Oh, by the way, I also learned to speak Spanish. I consider that an accomplishment because I didn't learn it until my 40s.

I have many interests and like to explore them all a little at a time. My love for what I do gives me the ability to enjoy each day as if it were just for fun.

CHAPTER 1

Why Should You Read This Book?

Ever wonder why one agent toils away without much success while another enjoys a thriving business?

Is it just luck? We talk about luck as though it were a living force — a force that chooses some people and ignores others. When you think about it, it's kind of silly to believe some force we can not even define decides who gets to be successful.

Is success based on talent? That is another word we use a lot without really understanding it. Is talent some mysterious quality people are "just born with?" And how does it affect success? We all know artists and performers who seem to have talent — whatever that is — but are not successful.

Researchers and thought leaders have discovered that success has more to do with preparation and opportunity than it does with mystical forces such as luck or talent. There is one thing you can count on when you combine opportunity with preparation...Success! When you know what to do and how to do it, your confidence builds and believe it or not confidence attracts opportunity.

That is what this book will teach you to do!

In real estate, you can prepare for success by increasing your knowledge of the market, practicing your people skills, differentiating yourself from competitors, training yourself to be a more effective negotiator, listening and internalizing motivational material and so much more.

You can create opportunities by looking for prospects in places other agents ignore, finding ways to meet more prospective buyers and sellers, and sharpening your marketing focus.

When your preparation intersects with opportunity, your success is not just more probable. It's inevitable.

There is a lot of competition in the real estate business. The National Association of Realtors® has a membership count of more than 2 million. That is a lot of real estate agents in the marketplace. The sheer quantity makes it hard for people who want to buy or sell homes to cut through the noise and find you. Everyone knows someone who is a real estate agent but not everyone knows a professional real estate agent who is successful in their career. Did you know that NAR states that 87% of all agents will quit within the first 5 years? To be a successful agent it takes more than just getting a license and hoping Aunt Jane or Uncle Larry will buy or sell with you.

This book will enable you to get business not just in spite of your competition, but because of it. You will learn how to develop superior skills and a Unique Selling Proposition that will get you more customers and make you more money. What you learn from reading this book will set you apart from other Realtors®. After reading through this book and doing the suggested work you will gain the following:

- Enable you to show customers why they should work with you instead of your competition.

- You will learn how to find your strengths and tell customers about them effectively — regardless of your communication style.

- You will discover how to build your clientele and take advantage of little-known principles such as the Law of 250.

- Provide you with tips on how to build your confidence, make friends, and become the kind of professional people want to work with.

- Learn how to communicate your values to customers, and prove it with testimonials, reviews, and case studies — *even if you're brand new to the real estate game!*

- Build your business plan, marketing plan to set you apart from every other Realtor®.

- Learn about an opportunity to not only be the go to agent in your market but build wealth and passive income in real estate without having to own any real estate.

Get ready to absorb no-nonsense tips on how to take your real estate business to the highest level. Every Realtor® is looking for an edge over their 2 million competitors. This book will provide you with that competitive advantage.

CHAPTER 2

An Overview of the 10 Steps

1. Show prospects how you helped other customers reach their goals. Customers do not have the knowledge of real estate to determine which agents are good and which are not. Most often, they use someone they know that is an agent. This is only because they already know, like and trust them. Use case studies and testimonials to prove your effectiveness. Case studies can be found by simply searching the internet for data. Do not worry if you have not had any transactions yet, you can use your broker or team's testimonials. Make sure to get permission first.

2. Make friends. People prefer to do business with people they know, like and trust. Win people's business by first getting to know them, develop conversation with them about things that interest them and build their trust by simply being genuine. Start by listening. People want to know you care and they know this by how attentive you are at what they are telling you. Repeat it back to them in your own words to help build that trust. Look for something about them that you admire and can compliment in a genuine way. Avoid focusing on possible areas of conflict or disagreement like religion or politics. This may sound elementary but there is much to be said about relationships and in today's world, with social media, it is so easy to create that trust.

3. Discover exactly why you're better. Identify the skills that set you apart from everyone else. If you have a problem with this, ask people who know you what skills and qualities you have that make you unique to them.

Your customers want to know why you are different. Just telling them is not going to convince them. Follow up with action. Show them why you are different. Make this an early highlight of conversation.

4. Be the confident professional. Is lack of confidence holding you back? Sell yourself to you first. Start by reviewing the ways you have helped others in the past. This does not have to be real estate related. It can be what you have done to help others in general. When you start to write it down, you will be impressed with yourself!

5. Sharpen your presentation. Practice makes perfect. If your presentation is still in development, find one online or ask your broker or team lead for a copy of theirs to help you get yours complete. It doesn't have to be perfect but your presentation of the plan needs to be part of natural conversation. This comes with practice and role playing with a colleague or a friend. It may feel a bit awkward but is necessary to get comfortable with what you will say and how you will flow through the presentation with confidence. This is paramount in getting the results you desire.

6. Create your Marketing Plan. You need a marketing plan.

Not just a generic marketing plan for clients but tailored buyer and seller plans. These are separate plans with specifics to market for sellers and buyers? What? How do you market for your buyers? You would be surprised how many agents overlook this important step! There are specific steps you need to take to set yourself apart for your buyers and find the right property for them. Knowing what you will do and how you will do it and presenting this to your buyers will definitely set you apart from the rest.

7. Find your passion and use it to get business. Customers are drawn to passionate people. You can integrate that passion into your real estate business. Doing this makes work more fun and enjoyable. This can also give you greater satisfaction by putting more of "you" in your career. People can see this in your work and will be drawn to you because of it.

8. Develop a niche and promote yourself as the expert. Clients want to work with an expert. Tap your unique expertise. Using this expertise to develop a Niche market will draw people to you in that niche because you have a unique interest in that area. People want to work with people who are experts.

9. Identify and use your communication strength. Different people communicate in different ways. Some are great public speakers. Some express themselves more effectively through their writing. Others are more comfortable communicating and building rapport one-on-one. Avoid your personal pitfalls and find the way that works best for you.

10. Build your clientele. Wouldn't you love to wake up every morning and know that new customers were on their way? Learn the secret of a top sales expert, who shared his secret, the Law of 250. The law of 250 principle is that most people have about 250 people in their lives who would show up at their funeral or wedding. There are exceptions, of course. Some have more, some have less. But the average seems to be 250. Make a list of everyone you know and start there. You already have the hard part out of the way...they know you.

BONUS: You can not only command your market but build a recession proof business that will provide you and your family peace of mind and passive income. Imagine being able to be a part of real estate anywhere in the world!

KEY TAKEAWAYS:

- This book details the 10 simple steps — and professional secrets — to unlocking skills you didn't know you had.

- Learning and applying the 10 steps detailed in this book will help you build a real estate business that is fulfilling, self-sustaining, and above all, successful.

CHAPTER 3

Show Prospects How You Helped Other Customers Reach Their Goals

You might have heard the adage, "Don't just tell people — show them!" It is a key to success in many industries and professions, from sales and marketing to filmmaking. Why? Because all of your competitors claim to help their clients. But very few know how to demonstrate it in a concrete, convincing way.

The best way to demonstrate your value to prospective customers — the best way to prove why they should work with you — is to give them testimonials and case studies of how you helped other customers reach their goals.

WHY DOES THIS MATTER?

Why do you need to give them testimonials and case studies? Let me explain. The average person does not know anything about real estate. They do not know the difference in a good or not so good

Realtor®. The plethora of information on the internet is contradictory and confusing to most.

Frankly, they do not understand real estate any more than you or I understand engine rebuilding, civil litigation, or heart surgery. If we were to go out and hire a mechanic to rebuild our engine, or a lawyer to defend us in a lawsuit, or a doctor to perform our heart surgery, we would not know much about the process.

It is no different for prospective real estate customers. Knowing who to trust with the biggest transaction they will ever make is a mystery to them. By giving them case studies and testimonials, you can show them why you are good and give them the confidence to work with you.

Making big claims about your abilities alone, will not be enough to win your prospects' trust. If they have had a bad experience with a real estate agent, or with any professional, they are likely to be skeptical.

With so many Realtors® to pick from and with Uncle Bob or Aunt Jane real estate agents, how do they know who to choose to work with?

HERE IS HOW TO DO IT

You can give prospects a case study. You can give them examples of how you sold a house, for example, that another agent was not able to sell. You can show them examples of how you were able to negotiate a better price for your customer. You can show them examples of how you were able to help another home buyer find their dream home, despite the obstacles. You can show them how you solved problems in a transaction. That is a case study.

Basically, you show the before and after. Before, there was a seller, and an agent could not sell their house. The seller did not know what to do. So, they hired you to sell their house, and you got it done, despite their earlier problems.

Here's an example of an effective case study:

Case Study #1: Home was for sale for 12 months with two other Realtors®. The sellers hired me, and I sold it in 8 days for 98.3% of the asking price.

This was an interesting sale. The sellers had been trying to sell the home for a year and really struggled at it. The reason the home wasn't selling was not because of the price. (The home was absolutely worth what the sellers were asking for.) BUT, there was a minor complication. The neighborhood where the home was located was considering some major upgrades.

They were considering assessing everyone in the neighborhood for $7,000 to $8,000 each to cover *the cost. The buyers would look at the house and then get cold feet because of the pending assessment.*

Most of the buyers would say something like, "I'll buy your house, but I want an $8,000 discount on the price because of the special assessment."

The sellers would reply, "I'm glad to sell you my house, but I am not going to discount $8,000 because we think the special assessment is not going to go through."

The sellers told me, the new agent, about the problem when they were putting the home up for sale. The agent thought about it for a few minutes and proposed a solution.

Here's what he told them:

"Let's sell the house and agree to hold $8,000 in escrow. If the special assessment goes through within a year, then the buyers get that $8,000. If it does not go through within a year, then the $8,000 goes to you."

They all agreed that it sounded like a good idea. The home sold very fast for 98.3% of the asking price. The $8,000 was put into escrow and an attorney typed up the escrow agreement.

It turned out that the sellers were correct. The opposition in the neighborhood was strong and the special assessment never went through.

A year later, the sellers received the $8,000 that had been put into escrow. This story gives you a great *example of some of the problems a good agent solves on a day-to-day basis.*

I don't think the agent's idea was particularly revolutionary, but it did solve the problem. Honestly, I am sometimes surprised at how little effort other people put into selling a home.

Here is a sample post and or ad you can use:
Do You Want to Sell Your Home
for More Money?
Give Me a Call Right Away
at (XXX) XXX-XXXX.

As you can see, case studies tell stories — stories about sales that have been accomplished. Stories about problems that have been solved. It is best if you put together a really good case study that proves how you were able to get a better result than the other agent who had been working on the problem.

Did you overcome an inherent weakness in the property? Identify a hidden advantage that the owners — and especially, other agents — completely overlooked? Help the buyers locate creative financing? Save what seemed like a doomed sale with a last-minute show of negotiating heroics? What sets you apart from the people who couldn't get it done?

USING VIDEO TESTIMONIALS

Here is another great way to put together testimonials for your business: use video testimonials whenever you go and meet with a customer to sign a contract.

Let's say you have a listing, and it's been on the market a while with another Realtor®, who was not able to sell it. You go meet with the sellers. You finally get an offer. You finally get a contract. You meet with them to sign the contract. While you are doing that, pull out your cell phone and get a testimonial video.

The closing is a great place to get a video testimonial. You are meeting with the seller to sign the contract, they will probably be on an emotional high.

Signing the contract is a high point, when both sides of the sale breathe a sigh of relief. It feels as though the hard work and anticipation have paid off, even though additional problems may surface.

Remember, problems are good. If there were not any problems, people would not need to hire a Realtor®. Do not be ashamed of problems but be careful to choose the right time to record your testimonial video. Wait until problems have been resolved. Then be ready to shoot an additional testimonial video after the closing, when final documents are signed and everyone is happy again.

OK, now that you know when to get your testimonial video, here is how to get it. Most people are not professional speakers. Even if you script their comments in advance, most people are not good speakers. I do not mean to sound harsh or to be rude to anybody, but it is just the reality. Most of us are not good speakers.

In order to get an effective testimonial, you are going to have to ask your customer questions. Ask "How long did you have your house for sale with the other Realtor® when it didn't sell?" They might answer, "I had my house for sale for three months."

Then, you ask them, "Were you frustrated during the process of three months when it wouldn't sell?" They might answer with something such as, "Yes, I was very frustrated for three months when the other agent could not sell my house." So far, so good.

Now, you can script those two things together and get the customer's answer, so they speak smoothly and convincingly. They can say good things about you, talk about the job you have done, but you will have to ask them questions and basically pull the testimonial out of them. Do not expect them to walk in the door and have an amazing testimonial ready for you.

Here are some questions you might consider asking:

- How did you feel?

- What were some of the low points?

- What were some of the high points?

- What do you think I did better?

- What do you think I did differently?

- Would you recommend me to any of your friends and family?

- Would you recommend other people work with me?

- Would you recommend people not work with the other agent? (Don't use the other agent's name!)

In this way, you will pull all the desirable information out of your client. Once you are done, you will want to go through and edit all that information into a solid, continuous testimonial, in which it sounds like only the client is talking. If you do not know how to do this, you can hire someone to edit the video for you on a website such as fiver.com or freelancer.com.

Here is another tip. When people are being interviewed for a testimonial, they usually do not know where to look. Hold your phone or camera close to your head, and just have the client look at you. This will seem more natural to them and will look much more natural in the finished video.

Nothing looks worse than a client who continually shifts focus, darting their eyes back and forth between you and the camera. This makes people look shifty and dishonest.

Pay attention to sound quality. If possible, record your client in a room that does not echo, and hold your phone close enough to them so that they can be heard plainly.

Smoothly edited video testimonials are very powerful tools for showing prospects how you've helped other customers solve their problems and reach their goals.

GETTING EMAIL TESTIMONIALS

The next thing you can think about doing is email testimonials. Handle these similarly to the way you handle video testimonials. Send your customer a list of questions:

Hey, John. I just sold your house. I really appreciate your business. By the way, would you mind answering a couple of questions for me?

- *Do you think I did a good job?*

- *Would you recommend me to your friends and family?*

- *How was the experience?*

- *How would you compare it with prior experience?*

Two or three of the right questions might be all you need. After they have answered all your questions, you will have information you can turn into a testimonial. Maybe you could write it into a sentence or a couple of mini-paragraphs. Then, send it back to the customer, and ask if they are OK with the final product. If they are, you are ready to use it.

You will be writing the testimonial for your customer. What you are really doing is you are pulling the testimonial out of them and scripting it, so that it reads really well.

ASK FOR REVIEWS

Once you have gone back and forth with your customer and completed their email testimonial, why not turn it into a review? Ask them if they will go online to Zillow or Realtor.com and post their comment in the review section.

Here are some other ways to get reviews. Again, a good time to get a review is when you sign the contract with the customer. For example, maybe you are working with a buyer. They have found their dream home, and they are negotiating the price.

Finally, the seller accepts their offer, and you are meeting with them to sign off on the contract. That is an emotional high and a great time to get a testimonial from that buyer, and it is also a great time to get the buyer's review.

You can ask for an additional review at the closing. Do not worry about asking for the review in the presence of the other agent. In a lot of cases, the other agent will jump in and get their own review from their customer. You can even offer to help them do that.

Remember, be gracious. Do not try to outshine anyone, and especially, do not say anything bad about the other agent in front of their customer. Just go ahead and get the reviews.

Bring your cell phone or laptop computer. Hook it up to Wi-Fi if it is available at the office where the closing takes place. Then, you can type the review into your computer with your customer or show them how to enter a review on Zillow or Realtor.com — even walk them through it on their cell phone.

FINAL TIPS FOR TESTIMONIALS

What if you are not yet a top producer? What if you are just starting out or don't have a bunch of reviews? What if you have no reviews or testimonials? Don't sweat it! You are not alone.

You can still use reviews, testimonials, and case studies. How? Use the case studies from your brokerage.

If you are just starting out and your broker is going to be helping you, then your broker will have case studies you can use. Use the case studies from other agents at your brokerage and the reviews of your brokerage to grow your business.

Remember, if a picture is worth a thousand words, then a testimonial can save you a thousand words trying to convince a customer to work with you.

KEY TAKEAWAYS:

- Most people do not understand real estate and cannot pick good agents from bad ones.

- Use case studies, testimonials, and reviews to show how you have helped other customers reach their goals.

- Contract signings and closings are great times to record testimonials on your cell phone and obtain reviews.

- Use questions to pull information from clients. Professional editing also helps.

- If you are a new agent or have no case studies or reviews, use your broker's.

CHAPTER 4

Make Friends

People like to do business with people they like!
You are likable! Just get out there and make friends.
Just be yourself and put yourself out there.

If you are not sure where to start then let's keep
reading. I will show you how.

ONE REALTOR'S STORY

This is a tru story about a man who struggled to
make friends. He wasn't very good at it, and he
honestly doubted that he had the ability to make
friends. Because he was a Realtor®, his struggle
held him back from his true potential in the real
estate business.

Once this man committed himself to learning the
necessary skills, he discovered there were some
excellent books and other resources at his command.
One of the best was Dale Carnegie's classic, *How to
Win Friends and Influence People*. Gradually, the
guy learned the steps in winning friends and began
applying the principles successfully.

It's interesting that the man in my example started by wanting to make friends so that he could become more successful in real estate. Today, this man loves real estate because it is a great way for him to meet people and make friends.

Dale Carnegie realized that people are largely emotional, not logical. Often, they are motivated by prejudices, pride, and vanity.

Carnegie advised his readers to arouse in the other person an eager want. The best way to influence others is to talk about what they want and show them how to get it. If there is one secret of success, it is the ability to see things the way the other person sees them.

Here is what you can do: just learn how to be nice. I know that sounds a little corny, but niceness matters. Just being nice can make a big difference to your business. Then you can learn how to bond with people.

To learn how to connect with people, find something that they are interested in and that you are interested in. As you learn these skills on how to make friends, you can practice by going to community events, interacting with people. There are many ways you can practice how to make friends.

Here are a couple of tips on things that you can do to make friends right away. The first thing you want to do is to become genuinely interested in other people. Learn how to listen to them. Learn how to let them talk for 5 minutes, 10 minutes, 20 minutes, 30 minutes, and just listen.

TIPS FOR MAKING FRIENDS

Break the Ice Gently:

- Become genuinely interested in other people.

- Smile and maintain good eye contact.

- Learn a person's name, remember it, and use it in the conversation.

- Listen attentively and encourage people to talk about themselves.

- Find a reason to give the other person a sincere compliment.

- Center your conversation around the other person's interests. Look for interests that you have in common.

- Make the other person feel like the most important person in the room.

Show Respect and Promote Engagement:

- Never argue. Be respectful of others' opinions. Don't say, "You're wrong."

- Nod your agreement with the other person. Try to phrase points so that they find it easy to say "yes."

- Let them do most of the talking and think they came up with the good ideas.

- Practice empathy, but don't say, "I understand how you feel" unless you've been in the same situation.

- Assume the other person has good intentions.

- When possible, tell stories to illustrate your points.

Avoid Friction:

- If the other person makes a mistake, call it to their attention indirectly. Ask for clarification — do not confront.

- Be quick to acknowledge your own mistakes.

- Avoid sounding dictatorial. Put what you want the other person to do in the form of a question: "Wouldn't you...?" or "That is acceptable, isn't it?"

- Help the other person save face. Never make them feel cornered or defensive.

Be interested in what they have to tell you. I can almost hear you asking, "But what if I'm really not interested?" Remember, it's a skill that you can develop.

Start by finding a way to be interested in what they are saying. Find the common ground in the subject so you can communicate with them and learn more. Part of being interested is just keeping yourself alert and engaged. Avoid being judgmental. You don't agree with everything your friends say, right? Just treat the people you meet the way you treat your friends or better yet, treat them the way you would like to be treated.

Once you learn this, you will see huge changes in customers. I have met with some people who came in and were kind of ornery, difficult to deal with, and even hostile. I let them first speak and tell me what is on their mind. Then I use what I have learned to craft a conversation that is all about them bringing it back to the end result which is selling their home with me.

You can do the same thing. It all starts with learning how to listen. You can try turning it into a contest for yourself. See how long you can let someone else talk before you open your mouth and speak. Maybe you meet a new person at a community event or somewhere or maybe a new customer. Just let them talk.

If you're there meeting them one-on-one, maybe at an open house, just let them talk and talk and talk. Just smile and listen to them and see how long you can go before you interrupt or reply.

Most people avoid silence. The less you say, the harder they will work to fill up the empty spaces in the conversation. Think of how much you will learn about the other person! You will learn what they like — things you can touch on to bond with them. You will learn their dislikes — things to avoid in future conversations.

You'll find out what they think about things — their hopes and goals, their fears and insecurities. All of these things help define your role as a friend. How can you help these people? How can you support their goals? How can you put them at ease?

You can train yourself to become a good listener. A good listener will run circles around somebody who talks a lot about themselves.

Engage with them only to acknowledge them and continue listening. Do not intervene even if they say something you disagree with or that sounds strange to you, learn to appreciate how and why they developed those ideas. It has been said that we learn the most from the people who are the least like us. Learning about the differences in people can be interesting.

Make the people you meet feel important and do it sincerely. Do not make them feel important with false flattery. Make them feel important because you take the time to really hear what they have to say. Make them feel important, and you are going to gain friends.

DON'T FORGET NONVERBAL CUES

Remember that nonverbal cues — the little behavioral signals we give to others — are often an important part of building friendship. Maintain eye contact with the person you meet — not a searing glare that makes them feel uncomfortable, but enough to let them feel that they have your undivided attention. Don't look around distractedly.

Watch your posture. If you are sitting far away from them, tensed up with your arms and legs crossed, you are probably sending the wrong message. Try opening up a bit, physically. Lean in toward them slightly, to make it clear that what they say is important for you to hear.

Many people find success by *mirroring* — watching the other person and trying to adopt the same posture, expressions, and gestures. This is a good idea, but do not make it so obvious that the other person thinks you're making fun of them.

When you speak — again, let them do most of the talking — keep your voice at an easy pace that's not too fast. Let people know you have time for what they want to say.

Smile. It is hard to dislike someone who clearly likes us. So, show outward signs that you like the other person.

A FEW LAST TIPS

Do not criticize what people have to say, their thoughts, or actions. Do not condemn them, and do not complain. Criticism is futile. It puts people on the defensive, which often leads to trying to justify themselves. Criticism wounds people's pride, damages their sense of importance, and arouses resentment.

You will show more character and self-control by being understanding and forgiving. Find any way that you can to give honest and sincere appreciation.

As Thomas Carlyle said: *A great man shows his greatness by the way he treats little men.*

KEY TAKEAWAYS:

- All other factors being equal, people prefer to buy from friends or individuals they like.

- Making friends is a skill anyone can learn. The more you practice being friendly, the better you will be at making friends.

- Start by being nice and a good listener. Let people talk, and do not judge them.

- Study great resources, such as Dale Carnegie's book, How to Win Friends and Influence People.

- To help you bond with someone, find something that person is interested in that also interests you.

- Make sure your nonverbal behavior is engaging. Keep your posture open, smile, maintain appropriate eye contact, and use a pleasant, medium-paced voice.

CHAPTER 5

Crafting and communicating your USP

Your USP (Unique Selling Proposition) is your key to opening a world of opportunity. Basically your USP is the reason you are different from other real estate agents. You tap into your strengths to develop a unique way for people to see you and what you do based on the way you do or want to do business. Why does this matter? Let me explain.

Great marketers know the value of market positioning. It's a strategy to make your brand or product stand apart from those of your competitors in the minds of your customers.

Remember those 1 million Realtors® we talked about earlier? It's important to set yourself apart from them, or at least the ones in your market area. What do you do that they don't? Why are you the best at doing it?

Most people do not know how to show prospective customers why they are better — even when they are much better than their competition. It is a reality of life. Some established businesses have more customers, have more traction in the marketplace just because they have been around longer. That doesn't necessarily mean that they're better.

Have you ever heard of Hewlett-Packard (HP)? At one time they were the best computer company around. They have been around the longest. Almost everybody in America knows who HP is. When Apple was created they were a small time nobody creating computers but they learned something very valuable. Set yourself apart from the others by magnifying what you do that is unique to you. The rest is history. Apple is the most recognized brand in the computer industry today.

We all know examples of people who did an amazing job but did not have a lot of customers because not enough people knew about them. I have seen examples in practically every industry. Often, people who do an amazing job just do not know how to tell people why they are better. I have even seen marketing people who are so busy doing great work for their clients that they forget to market themselves!

One problem is that even high-performing individuals usually do not know how to tell a story about their abilities. Stories are powerful. The best stories do not just give the facts — they make facts memorable by engaging listeners' emotions. Tell a story to back up your claim about why you're better and why the customer should work with you.

FOLLOW A 3-STEP PROCESS

This is how you can tell customers why you are better than your competition. The difference between you and your competitors does not have to be huge. Perhaps you're just better at a specific niche or better in a different way. Setting yourself apart from — and above — your competition is a three-step process:

1. Determine what makes you better. Write it down!
2. Plan how you will tell customers why you are better.
3. Test out your message and tweak it based on the response.

HOW TO DETERMINE WHAT MAKES YOU BETTER

Determining why you are better is not difficult. Before you get into fancy graphs and all sorts of analytics, just look at the basics. In marketing terms, this is all about developing your Unique Selling Proposition (USP). Remember when we talked about using testimonials? If you have testimonials and case studies, you already have proof that you are better. If you do not yet have testimonials, ask your friends and family what makes you unique. They will be happy to tell you.

This is what you can do: find something that separates you from other agents. It has to be believable. Here are a few ideas of differentiators you can look for in your own expertise.

Negotiating: Perhaps your business experience makes you an excellent negotiator. You used to work at a Fortune 500 company. Be aware that many agents claim to be good negotiators, so be prepared to explain your expertise to your prospects and customers in ways that are convincing and easy to understand. Offer them proof.

Tell your customers stories about the multi-million-dollar deals you negotiated. Give them examples of deals you initiated because you dug into research your competitors overlooked. Tell them about the time you lightened a tense negotiation by telling a well-timed joke.

Give people inside information about the negotiation process — how to know when to be flexible or stand firm on pricing. Explain how to know when a buyer or seller is bluffing. Connect your skills to results that are meaningful to the customer — usually making or saving them money. Tell them how you are an excellent negotiator who will negotiate a better deal for them whether they are buying or selling a house.

Customer Service: If you have worked in customer service, tell people about that. "Hey, I know how to take care of customers and keep them happy. Come to me for a world-class customer experience!" Tell them you will save them time, money, and frustration by anticipating their needs. You will take the worry out of a real estate transaction by explaining things in simple terms, not jargon. Prove what you say with testimonials, reviews, and ratings from satisfied customers or from past clients who

Perhaps you worked in a non-real estate job, such as waiting tables. Tell people you're used to a fast-paced environment, solving problems, and resolving complaints from difficult people. You're an expert at keeping people happy.

Were you an account rep? Talk about your problem-solving skills, attention to detail, employee-of-the-month awards, and how you earned customer loyalty.

Are your clients selling homes in an upscale community? Explain that you know what makes upscale professionals and business owners "tick" — the same people likely to buy their home.

Did you work in retail? Talk about your customer-first attitude, thinking on your toes, and how you are willing to put in long hours to make a sale. You are used to dealing with unique requests and providing high-level customer service.

Staging Houses: Maybe your talent is visualizing a home from the buyer's point of view. You understand how the right paint job, furnishings, and carpeting can maximize a home's advantages — and minimize problems. Talk about how effective staging sells homes for more money. Provide a few hints of how you might stage their home — just enough to let them see the possibilities.

Even if you are not a full-blown "stager," you can communicate your passion for staging. Have you worked as an artist, graphic designer, or interior designer? Have you sold — or made — furniture? Worked in a paint store mixing colors? Any of these experiences can be turned into an advantage in staging. Perhaps you can save the sellers money by staging their home instead of having an expensive professional do it.

Maybe you stay up-to-date on the latest trends. Perhaps you simply know the best local stagers and contractors. If you are working with buyers, let them know how your staging expertise will help them turn their house into a home.

Photographing Houses: Talk about how you will take better-quality, more appealing pictures of their house. Everybody says, "A picture is worth a thousand words." Why not talk about that? "Hey, instead of writing an ad about your house having four bedrooms and three baths, I can take an amazing picture that will capture attention and make buyers instantly fall in love with your house!" You could also take pictures of your prospect's home and post them on Instagram to attract buyers.

Talk about how your expert lighting composition will showcase their home's best features, making their house sparkle and shine. With a little research, you can find examples of similar homes that sold well with good-quality photos or languished on the market with amateur-looking pictures.

Marketing: If you used to work in media or at an ad agency, then talk about your marketing expertise and how you will use it to do a better job of selling their house. If you have worked in real estate a while, you probably have examples of how you have done this better than your competitors. Perhaps you write brilliant ad copy, or you network extensively with local professionals.

What If You Were a Chef? If you have worked as a cook or a chef, talk about your kitchen expertise. You could talk about your ability to handle important details under pressure. Who better than a former chef to explain to buyers the advantages of an efficient kitchen, energy-saving appliances, or an outdoor grilling area? Perhaps sharing a few recipes would inspire future owners. Maybe instead of chocolate chip cookies, your canapés would make an open house the talk of the town.

You Worked in Construction: Maybe you used to work in construction. You know more about the quality craftsmanship and materials of the home than other agents. In fact, maybe you could specialize in new construction, because you are used to working with builders and contractors.

Make sure to stress you are not an inspector so you won't assume liability for problems. But you can certainly point out the strengths and weaknesses of a home, and alert sellers — or buyers — to potential problems before expensive repairs are needed.

You Understand Financing: Maybe you used to work in lending. In that case, you could talk about your lending expertise, how you can make sure your clients are getting the best deal on their financing, how you can make sure that sellers will have a less stressful sale. As you probably know, financing is the number one cause of stress in real estate.

Other Ideas: I know of a home painter who went into real estate. Strange as it seems, he worked both of these very different jobs at the same time. He would offer to paint the sellers' house if they would list their home with him! He got several listings this way.

Examples are endless. Remember, your niche might be your passion, rather than your expertise. Are you passionate about fishing? The beach? Waterfront properties? Historic districts? Whatever matters to you, it gives you an opportunity to communicate with prospects and clients on uniquely engaging terms. (I'll explore this in more depth later in the book.)

You can literally "speak their language" and use that ability to bond, to earn their trust, and achieve success on their behalf. You can be the person they want to sell their house.

TELLING YOUR CUSTOMERS

Once you have figured out why you are better than your competitors, it is up to you to capitalize on that difference by communicating it to customers. Here are a couple of tips on how you can tell customers why you're better.

Whenever you are talking to a customer, get straight to the point on how you can benefit them. Do not say, "Ben, I notice you are looking for a home at the beach, and I love the beach. I just love living here in Atlantic Beach," blah, blah, blah, and, "I love living here in this beach town," blah, blah, blah.

Instead, you can say, "I specialize in beach properties," or, "I'm an expert at beach properties." Get straight to the point on how you can benefit them. "I'm an expert at better marketing that will sell your house for more money." "I'm an expert at negotiating a better price for your house."

Remember, the faster you tell them how you can help them, the better. Drag out your message too long, and people just conk out. They stop paying attention and say, "You know what? I'm not interested," and they do not talk to you anymore.

You only have 10 seconds to make a great first impression. So, make sure your first impression is quick, and get to the point of why they should work with you as quickly as possible.

Another example: If you have a great customer service background, you could say, "I specialize in great customer service. I used to be a customer service expert at ABC Corporation, and I got a top-notch rating because of my customer service abilities."

Now that you have crafted your USP and have got it down to 10 seconds you can use it and watch your business begin to grow.

AVOID THESE MISTAKES

Remember that you are unique and offer something that no other agent offers. Do not fall into the trap of the same old routine that other agents are using just because someone says it is the latest and greatest. What works for one agent may not work for another

At one time, there were many car dealer radio advertisements and TV commercial? Every single car dealer ad said the same thing: "We have the lowest prices. We will not be beat. Our prices are so low." they did it because studies showed those things worked to compel customers to come to their dealership. All it really did was put that dealer in the same pool as all the other dealers saying the same thing. They just blended into the monotony of the lowest price that will not be beat.

Let's imagine we actually have a car dealership that has the lowest prices. Who cares? The problem is, everybody claims to have the lowest prices, but the consumer cannot sort out whose prices are lowest. With every single car dealer claiming to have the lowest prices, it does not matter if you genuinely do have the lowest prices, because you appear no different from everyone else. If you were to change your ad to say something different, like with. all the low prices out there, we can give you our price guarantee, "Buy ours and if you find the same model somewhere for less we will refund the difference." Get your attention? See the difference?

TIRED CLICHES

Here are some of the claims I have noticed real estate agents make. If you claim to have these same things, it may be hard to stand out from your competition.

"I am available 24/7, 365 days a year!" A lot of agents say things such as this. I am available anytime. Call me at 2 in the morning, and I will answer the phone."

"I have the best service!" In fact, this claim is kind of sad. I honestly feel bad, but I know of a real estate company that started up — it was actually a real estate team — and they talked about how they had the best service. That was everything they talked about.

Their branding was so pitiful that they ended up having to change the name of their company. Maybe they did have the best service — I don't know. The fact is, it did not matter to consumers. It did not get the company any business.

"I return phone calls!" (Yawn!) A lot of agents seem to like to talk about the fact that they return phone calls. Does anyone just sit and stare at the phone when it rings? Does any real estate agent with even minimal confidence and enthusiasm not return customers' calls?

"I know the area!" I would suggest avoiding saying this, because almost everybody claims to know the area. If you claim to know the area, make sure you follow up immediately with proof. Study your area to learn all you can about it — the demographics, income levels, offering prices and actual sales prices, sales trends, shopping, schools, and, well, everything else.

Make sure your selling proposition is unique. If it is not different from everyone else's, then it won't help you stand out. And if you don't stand out from your competition, you are just part of the background noise. That is not the way to grow your business.

KEY TAKEAWAYS:

- Identify the passion, experience, or skill that sets you apart from competitors.

- Communicate it well to increase your business.

- You have 10 seconds or less to make a great first impression on prospects.

- When communicating, avoid clichés that make you sound like all the other agents.

CHAPTER 6

Be the Confident Professional Clients Want to Hire

Sell yourself on you. Now, what do I mean by that? I mean that a big part of performing anything well is gaining the confidence that you can do it. You have to first sell yourself — you — on why you are a great Realtor®, and why you deserve people's business.

We all know that confidence makes a huge difference for any business person or professional. Imagine how you would react if your doctor acted nervous and uncertain when describing the heart surgery you were about to undergo! If you're confident, you have a way better chance at getting the business.

Besides being confident, there are a couple of other things you can do. Why does this matter? Why do you need to sell yourself on you first before you try to sell other people on you?

HELPING CUSTOMERS DECIDE

The average real estate customer does not know who is a good agent and who is not. They do not understand real estate, so they have no basis for choosing an agent.

In addition, everyone has qualms. They have been burned by a business. They have been lied to by people who are trying to sell them something. As a result, they are skeptical and they are cautious. You have to convince them you are the right choice, and part of that is showing them that you are confident.

Think about your own experiences. Think about the last time you hired somebody to work on your car. You took it to a mechanic. Unless you have worked with that car mechanic or repair shop for years, and they have proved themselves over and over, it is hard for you to have confidence that they are good at what they do.

Now, if they show you testimonials, positive reviews, or you have been referred to them by several of your friends, you will have confidence in that car repair shop. But what if there are no testimonials, reviews, or referrals? If you are just talking to them, they can be the best in the world, but you just cannot be sure.

You have the opportunity to show you are reliable by providing proof from prior customers or your broker. You can also use referrals from friends and family if you do not yet have your own referrals and testimonials.

CUSTOMERS ARE OVERWHELMED

Even if customers are not skeptical about your abilities, there are so many real estate agents out there, it is confusing to know which one to pick. When you have the opportunity to talk with a prospective customer, whether it is by phone or face-to-face, it is important to be confident.

Your confidence tells them several important things about yourself. First, it tells them that you are comfortable. You are in control of the situation. You can handle things. You have been in this situation before. You are a seasoned professional — even if, in reality, you are new to the game of real estate!

Your confidence tells them that you believe in yourself. You are not nervous and twitchy, like somebody who doubts their own motives or weaknesses or has something to hide. People who are trustworthy and have good character are confident in themselves. All of these things tell the client they should choose to work with you.

The agent who is sold on why he or she is better probably is better, and as a result, the customers will probably work with that agent.

HOW TO BUILD YOUR CONFIDENCE

Here is how you can sell yourself to yourself. Go look at some of your testimonials. Remember I talked about testimonials in Chapter 2 of this book? Read through your testimonials. Remember the stories and think about them.

Think about the happiness you brought to families, the problems you solved for them, and the excellent customer service you provided. Then dig into the specifics. Look at past examples of how you got your customers a better deal.

Many of your competitors claim to be top agents who sell homes for more money. Check out their list of sale prices. Check out your list of sale prices. See how your list of sale price compares with other agents and with other companies.

When you do this, when you start to go through some of your past sales, you are going to feel a sense of confidence. When you stop to focus on good things you have accomplished, and the good things grateful people have said about your work, you cannot help but be proud and confident.

Every testimonial or positive customer review is an affirmation — a statement that someone believes in you. A statement that you've proved your value. A reinforcement of the fact that you deserve to be confident about your work in real estate.

These are not just "feel-good" statements, either. They are concrete examples of your hard work, your skillful effort, and your dedicated customer service.

Think about the homes you sold or the buyers you helped find for those sellers. Compare your average list to sale price with other agents. Look at some of the deals you were able to negotiate on behalf of your buyers.

Perhaps you were more effective because you were a better listener, who made your customers' needs your priority. Maybe you were better at returning phone calls and responding to emails. Or perhaps you put in extra time showing houses or researching the market.

The basics are important. If you know you covered the fundamentals well for your clients, then you can be confident that you do a really good job.

If you do not have those reviews this is what I recommend. On a sheet of paper begin to write all of your accomplishments from the beginning of your memory. Examples are, riding a bike, learning to play an instrument, getting your first job, and the list goes on and on. All of those accomplishments will build your self confidence, even though they seem insignificant. Seeing them all on one sheet of paper becomes impressive in itself.

KNOW YOUR MARKET

It is important to know the market you are working in. Even if you are new to the area, you can study area maps, chamber of commerce, local activity centers and drive through neighborhoods to become familiar with them. Visit as many open houses as you can and get general knowledge of the price range and condition of the homes. Become an expert on it. Whenever you have a customer, you will be able to assist them with ease because of your knowledge. That will also build your confidence and the customer can see that.

Learn the ins and outs of the neighborhoods. According to a study by the National Association of Realtors®, 78 percent of home buyers said neighborhood quality means more to them than the size of the home. In the same study, 57 percent of buyers preferred a shorter commute to having a larger yard.

What do people in your marketplace do for a living? Are they older, established professionals? Are they retirees looking to hit the golf course? Or are they people beginning their careers? Are they empty-nesters or folks just starting families? What is their average income?

Know the local home prices. Are they trending up or down? What are the construction styles? Who are the good builders? The bad builders? How are homes in the area usually financed? What are the local amenities, the schools, shopping areas, parks, and recreation activities? Research the trends. Know everything you can about your marketplace.

With every fact you learn about your marketplace, you will be building your confidence. You will be secure in the knowledge that you can answer any question from a seller or prospective buyer.

Everything you can learn about your marketplace is a potential advantage over competitors, a possible edge that differentiates you from other Realtors® in the minds of your customers.

GO ABOVE AND BEYOND

Part of confidence and capability is commitment, your willingness and determination to do the absolute best you possibly can for your client. To go above and beyond the good customer service that is reasonably expected of you.

Make it a goal to do this for the next 5 or 10 customers, and you will have way more confidence in serving all your customers in the future. Customer service is like a muscle — the more you exercise your good customer service, the more it grows.

Commitment can build your confidence, even if you are new to the real estate business and have not had much success yet. Just knowing that you will not settle for providing second-rate customer service will give you a confident attitude. You will meet every new customer, knowing that you are going to provide what that individual needs to be successful.

If you were a prospective real estate client, who would you choose to trust with your business? The agent who is obviously nervous and uncertain when explaining why he or she would like your business? An agent who is practically begging for your business?

Or would you choose the confident agent? The one who is already researched your marketplace? The one who can show you testimonials and online reviews? The one who clearly believes he or she can do the job and provide you with better customer service? Which one is the confident professional you want to hire?

VALUE YOURSELF

Then, once you have gone through this, put a higher value on yourself. Start thinking of yourself as a top producer, as someone who deserves the customer's business. Visualize success, not just in general, but also before every client meeting.

Do not fall into the trap of being intimidated by successful people. Realize that every single prospect, no matter how successful they are, has experienced many of the same struggles and insecurities.

I am not saying to go out there and envision them having struggles or insecurities. Just realize that most people face adversity and struggle with confidence at some point in their lives, no matter how successful they are...even those "top producers."

Also remember that highly successful individuals — even powerful CEOs — usually understand the value of working with specialists like you. Their ability to efficiently manage the strengths of others is one reason they became successful.

KEY TAKEAWAYS:

- Few people understand real estate. Most have had bad business experiences. They have trouble choosing a good agent from the many available.

- Showing confidence will help you get their business, but first, you must "sell" yourself.

- Reading your client testimonials and good reviews can inspire your confidence.

- Commit to providing excellent customer service and understanding your marketplace.

- Knowing that you are well prepared — and learning to value yourself — leads to success.

CHAPTER 7

Sharpen Your Presentation

So, why should you practice your presentation? The more you practice your presentation, the better you are going to be at giving it to potential customers. If you have a good presentation on why buyers should work with you to buy a house, and you practice it, you will get better and naturally convert more of those buyers into your clients.

Same thing with sellers. If I told you that potentially you could earn thousands of dollars and get more prospects to list their houses with you, just by practicing your listing presentation, why would you not do it? Well, that is exactly what I am telling you. You are getting paid to practice!

Here is the thing. Most people talk themselves into thinking they are not good at giving listing presentations. They tell themselves, "I'm a terrible presenter. I don't even try to do a presentation. I just try to bond with people and build rapport."

Well, yes, bonding and building rapport are good ideas, and you can practice both of those things and become better at them. But even if you decide to do that, you should still practice your presentation. Let's focus on practicing that listing presentation and why it is so important.

Most people who struggle with their presentations begin with the assumption that they do not have the natural, God-gifted talent to do it. That is not true. Let me give you a real-life example of why "natural talent" does not always matter in why you would be good at something.

Have you ever heard that most pro hockey players were born in a certain part of the year? Here is the deal: most pro hockey players are born in the first three months of the year, and many more are born in January than in any other month.

THE JANUARY FACTOR

Why in the world are the largest number of pro hockey players born in January? Shouldn't all the kids born in December, November, October, June, or May have the same skills on average, the same natural talent on average as the other hockey players? Why in the world are those other kids not being chosen to play professionally?

Scientific study has found that National Hockey League teams prefer to draft players born in the first quarter of the year — January through March. In fact, between 1980 and 2007, 36 percent of players drafted by NHL teams were born in the first quarter — January to March — compared to only 14.5 percent who were born in the fourth quarter — October to December.

Here is why. In Canada — the cradle of professional hockey — kids are selected for all-star teams at an early age. But the cutoff date for eligibility is December 31st. So, if you are born December 31st, you are going to play hockey with kids who are 10, 11, almost 12 months older than you.

Kids born closer to January 1st will have many natural advantages over kids born late in the year. They are bigger, faster, more experienced, and more mature. January kids are more likely to be singled out for all-star teams, where they will get more practice and play more games and get more experience playing on the road. Coaches will invest more time and effort into training them. They will also play against more talented, better-seasoned competitors.

As the January kids get older and advance through higher levels of competition, the advantages are compounded. By the time the players born in January reach draft age, they are thought to be more talented, when in reality, they've just had greater opportunities to develop their skills and confidence. As a result, they are more likely to become professional hockey players.

If talent were really the main factor, you would see professional hockey players whose birthdays were scattered more or less evenly all throughout the year, not primarily in the first quarter.

Now, think about your own success. Have you been losing lots of listing presentations? Maybe you are not a terrible presenter, after all. Maybe you could be an awesome, amazing presenter if you just practiced a little bit more. Refine your presentation. Refine your bio presentation. Refine your elevator pitch — the primary reason that somebody should work with you to buy or sell a house.

The more you practice, the better you will become, and you will also be able to adjust and improve your presentation. Maybe you will notice that if you say things a certain way, people immediately nod and think, "You know what, you sound like a great Realtor®. I want to work with you to sell my house."

Maybe you will identify where your presentation routinely goes wrong — gets too complicated, too filled with real estate jargon, or makes people look puzzled or unhappy. I bet you have heard the old saying, "Practice makes perfect." It is true.

Here is another reason why you should practice. Look at Tiger Woods. He practices like a maniac, 6, 8, 10 hours a day. Personal problems and bad health have eaten away at his concentration and skill level. But when Tiger Woods was at the top of his game, he was the best golfer in the world by a wide margin, and he got that way by practicing more intensely than anyone else.

Michael Jordan became a legend in professional basketball the same way — through intense practice. Lots of people who have reached the top of their industry, whether sports or business or entertainment, have gotten there not because they were naturally skilled. They took the skills they had and got ahead by practicing. And if you do have natural skills and abilities, imagine how much better you can become if you take the time to practice those skills and hone those abilities.

WHAT IS YOUR VALUE PROPOSITION?

Keep in mind that when you are speaking to a prospective client by phone or face-to-face, you do not have to be better than every real estate agent in the United States. Most home sellers do not interview 10 Realtors® to sell their house. They might interview just three Realtors®. If you practice, all you have to do is impress your prospects more than they are impressed by the other two or three agents they are interviewing. One important thing to remember is that NAR studies show that the home owner typically chooses the first agent that presents to them. If you are practiced and good at your presentation, you will be the one!!

Remember that the main point of an interview is to tell customers why they should work with you to buy or sell a house. In the previous chapter we learned about USP. Use it to your advantage in the presentation. It is what makes you different, and most important, it is what makes you better than your competition.

So, practice how you say it. Try changing words around just a little bit. The more practice, the better you are going to get at explaining to people why they should work with you to sell or buy a house. You will get to the point more quickly, without seeming pushy. You will make your points smoothly, without seeming too slick. Every engagement will feel more like a conversation than a speech.

Listen for people's feedback and incorporate it into your practice. What do you say that gets a good reaction and makes people say, "You know what? That makes sense. I can tell you are a great agent." Edit your presentation for clarity and also for economy — you want to make your point early and quickly, without seeming rushed.

Give your presentation to the mirror. Give your elevator pitch on why someone should work with you to sell or buy a house. Try your "elevator pitch" when you are riding alone in an elevator! Hahaha!

Talk to your spouse, partner, or maybe a supportive friend. Just talk to an actual person and get feedback from them. Do not get discouraged if they do not give you good feedback. Every opportunity you take to practice makes you a little bit better, a little bit more confident, than you were before.

Here is another method you can try. Record your presentation on audio or — better yet — on video. Let it sit there for a couple of days and then watch it with fresh eyes. It might take a few minutes to get used to the sound of your own voice. You are accustomed to hearing your voice through your bones and ear canals — everyone thinks they sound different on a recording.

People also tend to focus on what they think is wrong with their looks. Remember that a big part of looking confident is looking comfortable.

Uncertainty and self-doubt make us tense and jittery, which can give our faces a pained expression. A confident person looks relaxed — looks as though he or she belongs wherever they are.

Concentrate on what you say and whether you look and sound sincere and natural. You might find that you should say something differently in some places or avoid saying something in other places.

Gradually, you will get a much better presentation for listing appointments, a much better presentation for buyer appointments, and you are going to have more customers. Additionally, it will be easier and more pleasant for you. No one wants to feel that you are just using a hard close or coercing them into wanting to work with you. You do not want to feel that way, either.

Ideally, customers will think, "You know what, I can tell that you will do a great job in helping me find a perfect house." The things you are saying are obviously different from other real estate agents. You have a unique method that works better than anyone else. So just practice it, refine it, and you are going to grow your business.

KEY TAKEAWAYS:

- Practicing your presentation will help you fix any problems in advance.

- Focus on clarity and getting to the important points of why customers should work with you.

- Practice in front of a mirror, spouse, partner, or a supportive friend.

- Record yourself on video and watch it.

CHAPTER 8

Create Your Plan and Present it to Customers

Everyone talks about plans. Making a plan helps you to become focused on the goal. Let's talk about listings in this scenario, although it works just as well when working with buyers. You can make a plan for what you are going to do to help someone sell their house, or what you are going to do to help someone buy a house.

You might find this surprising, but most Realtors® do not make any plans or they are not complete and lack the necessary elements to show your prospective seller that you are the one to sell their house or a buyer that you are the one to help them buy their house. Many agents just meet with the seller and talk a lot. They do a great job of bonding and building rapport, and with a little bit of luck, they walk out, and they have got the listing.

Below is the method to help you separate yourself from other Realtors® who either have no plan — or do not have a great plan — like the plan you are going to have after you finish this chapter. Ready?

PROVE IT IN BLACK AND WHITE

Demonstrate what you can do on paper (or on your tablet screen, if that's how you present). Put together a checklist of what you do, and you also need to do a comparison. Ever seen one of those online comparisons, where a computer or software company compares what they do to what the average person or competitor does? You can do a checklist or a comparison sheet like that. Below is a shortened, simplified example of this format.

CREATE A MARKETING PLAN FOR LISTINGS

Regardless of the form you choose, here is how to put together a great marketing plan for listings. List all the things you are going to do:

- Put a sign in the yard.

- Advertise the property on Realtor.com.

- Advertise the property on Homes.com, Trulia.com, Zillow.com, and syndicate with over 100 other websites,

- Have professional pictures taken,

- Make a unique selling proposition for your house.

Now I want to show you what you put on the top of the list because the list above is whatever other agent is doing.

- I will sell your home in XX days. Use the average market days for the area that the home is in.

- Your Home will sell for XX% of the listed price. (Use your own percentages or your brokers if you don't have a percentage yet) Show a comparison to what the MLS % is and use a home in the price range of theirs to show how much money it will make them by listing with you

- Create a POWER PLAN to sell the home that includes staging, photos, advertising, Open House

- Discuss the 10 ways to sell your home quickly that other agents don't know about or rarely use.

- Initiate our VIP Client Services that guide you through the stress of selling your home.

- Initiate the marketing to our current list of buyers before your home goes on the market

- Market your home to a new list of buyers that we will generate through an aggressive marketing plan.

- Market your home to other agents in our area before your home goes on the market. This creates frenzy.

- and the list goes on

I am sure you can see the difference in these and the list above.

First, whenever you meet a prospective client, it will be easy for them to see that you are not a fly-by-night real estate agent who just shows up and does whatever comes to mind. You will show yourself to be a Realtor® with a solid plan that is going to give clients a better chance at selling their houses — or selling their houses for more money. Second, you can customize your marketing to the seller's needs.

CRAFT YOUR PLAN TO YOUR CUSTOMER

Let's say that you are meeting with a special seller. Perhaps she wants to sell a high-end home. You can tailor your marketing plan to show your effectiveness at selling to high-end buyers. Provide some data on potential buyers who would likely be interested — and qualified — to purchase the buyer's home. What would high-end purchasers find attractive about the neighborhood? What are the features of her home that would appeal to those high-end buyers? How would you communicate those features to them?

What are the homes like in the area that are likely to provide competition for upscale buyers? Where do they work, shop, or send their children to school? What kind of advertising would you use to capture the interest of those buyers? What are the most effective channels for getting the message out? Where and how would you market the seller's home to reach those buyers and attract their interest?

CLIENTS LIKE TO BE INCLUDED

You do not want sellers to feel like they are just another number — everybody deserves good service. If you are committed to providing that high level of service, be prepared to customize your marketing plan to the seller's needs.

Sellers like to feel included, so help them feel included. Show them what they can do to help the marketing and sales process. If they do not want to do any of the work, show them how you can handle it all, and ask for their input. For example, you could ask a seller, "What do you think needs to be done to sell this house?" One of the things that I like to ask them is what were the things that made them buy the house. This is often the same thing you can use to market the property.

You never know — they might have helpful insights and suggestions. There was one or more things that they like about the house when they purchased it that others will also like.

If they have any useful ideas, incorporate them into your plan. This will show them that you are a good listener, and if you do use any of their ideas, they'll feel more involved and engaged. That means you are more likely to get a listing.

Remember that for many people, a real estate transaction might be part of a bigger goal or dream. Buying a home might symbolize expanding their family, retiring, creating a home-based business, or attaining status.

Selling a home might be part of a plan to fund their kids' college education, downsize, or simplify their life. There could be as many reasons for buying and selling as there are buyers and sellers. The more you know about your prospective customers and the realities of their market, the more closely you can tailor your plan to fit their needs.

When possible, craft your plan around what they want. You can steer them in the right direction if they need a little help, but don't be too pushy.

DON'T FORGET THE BUYER

You also can put together a plan for a buyer. Here is how I would do it. I would look for every single home on the market that fits the buyer's criteria and tell them about it as soon as it comes on the market. I would put together an email alert to get those listings to the buyer ASAP.

Remember Chapter 5, where we talked about going above and beyond for our customers? I would look at homes that expired three months ago, and I would contact those sellers to see whether they are interested in selling their house. I would contact builders to see if they have any homes in the area that might fit what the buyer is looking for. I am willing to do whatever it is that is going to give that buyer an advantage over all the other buyers in the market looking to buy a house.

WHAT YOUR COMPETITORS IGNORE

You would be surprised how many agents never do this. They just say, "Hey, I do the standard stuff, I will help you buy a house, I will help you buy a house for the lowest price, etc."

If you have an actual, tangible plan for people to see, it is not just you "puffing" the goods and how great you are. Instead, you are sending the message, "I am going to follow this plan to find the right home for you at the best possible price."

KEEP IT SIMPLE

Your plan does not need to have a hundred things you are going to do. That is not always what is necessary, and customers cannot absorb that much information, anyway. It is better to include key items that will capture their attention. Most important, you need to include the things that you are going to do that are different or better than your competitors. Remember, the point is to prove you can help the seller — or buyer — get a better result.

Do not make the mistake of thinking that a list of a to-do list that takes up 10 pages — is going to impress your client. Be creative but do not fill the presentation with filler. Be precise and to the point. You will distract your client if they have to read through a long laundry list of things.

Apart from the distraction, a long list with too many items will become unbelievable. Strategic, on point items that move the needle in homes sales is all you want your list to contain. 20-30 points is sufficient.

One last tip is to name each process, like I showed you in the bullet points above. VIP Client Services, Power Plan, etc.

KEY TAKEAWAYS:

- Creating a marketing plan and sharing it with clients provides tangible evidence you know what you're doing.

- Keep your plan simple. List the important steps — the ones you'll do differently or better than your competitors.

- Customize your plan for specific needs of sellers and buyers. When practical, include their input.

- Name your processes to make them unique to you

CHAPTER 9

Find Your Passion and Use it to Get Business

People prefer to do business with individuals who are passionate about what they do. Don't believe me?

Think about one of your bad customer service experiences — perhaps a recent time you ordered dinner at a restaurant or stood in line waiting for someone to ring up your groceries at the supermarket.

There is no feeling worse than if you are standing in front of someone who should be attending to your need, like the check out at the store and they are really having a bad day, evident that they are not wanting to be there.

Now think of a really good customer service experience you had. Chances are your server or clerk greeted you with a smile and a friendly voice. They were alert, energetic, and moved quickly. They answered your questions promptly — even volunteered useful information — because it was clear that they knew their products and services well and they were glad to be there. They probably gave you a hearty "Thank you!" Now, how did that make you feel?

Ever go to one of those computer stores with the resident "experts?" Those people live and breathe their products. Are you a self-proclaimed computer "geek?" Do you spend your evenings playing video games and fall asleep reading a review of the latest software or smartphone app? Then you probably realize that the local computer store isn't just a shop — it is a community.

I would rather work with a Realtor® who is passionate than work with a Realtor® who is half dead. I know that is a horrible example, but people want someone who is passionate. They know if you are passionate about something, you are going to work harder, you are going to care, you are going to offer better, more educated opinions, and they are going to get a better result with selling or buying a house.

WELCOME TO AFFINITY MARKETING

Let me explain how this works and how you can use this to grow your business. Have you ever heard of Salt Life? Salt Life is a clothing brand. Basically, it is a brand that talks about salt life — enjoying life in the water, whether you're boating or fishing or whatever else salt life is all about.

As you can see, I do not know that much about salt life, but that is the power of affinity marketing. People will buy Salt Life shirts because they want to be part of Salt Life's community.

Now, if someone is interested in salt life, for example, they are more likely to hire a Realtor® who's into salt life. Maybe that Realtor® is an expert in boating and at least owns a boat, knows all the ins and outs of the different areas — they will know the best place to buy a house if you have a boat or how to sell a house that has a boat storage?

They are going to be passionate when they are marketing a house that has a boat storage or is on the water. Those are just a few of the possible examples of how you, as a Realtor®, might use affinity marketing. If you are passionate about something, you are going to be able to get more business by tapping into the spirit and interests of like-minded buyers and sellers.

Here are examples of some of the ways people could feel that you are one of them or feel connected to you. Let's look at salt life again, but in this case, I mean fishing. You could be really into fishing, and as a result, you could help sell or buy more fishing houses — houses that have a boat, are on the water, or near the water.

You could be very passionate about the outdoors, in general. If you like getting outside and running and jogging — whatever it is that gets you outdoors — you could talk about that and use it as a springboard for building a business rapport.

You could be passionate about country living. Who wants to live in a tiny little house in the middle of town with no yard when you can live on acreage in the country and enjoy nature? Country living is a rich tapestry of activities and interests. It embraces everything from living a simpler lifestyle to canning, quilting, rustic arts and crafts, home cooking, woodworking, and keeping and raising animals. If you are passionate about country living, that's something you could use to get more business from people who are buying or selling a country house.

Beach property is another great example. Some people love to live at the beach. If you are passionate about the beach, you understand exactly why it is worth paying the extra money to live where you can wake up to the sound of the waves breaking on the beach, enjoying long walks on the sand, and exploring every shell and piece of driftwood. If that describes you, then you are going to do a better job at helping buyers and marketing houses that are at the beach.

Same thing for golf — if you are into golf and you know the easiest courses, the most challenging holes, the best views, and the most sumptuous cocktails at the "19th hole," you could get a lot of business from the golf niche because you understand them. It will be much easier to relate to your client so helping them accomplish their goal will be easier and more enjoyable for you.

EXPRESS YOURSELF

The late George Carlin was a polarizing force in standup comedy. No one can deny his success and groundbreaking influence on the entertainment industry. Carlin made it on television in the 1960s, mostly portraying zany onstage characters, such as "Al Sleet, the Hippie-Dippie Weatherman." He was getting work and making money, but he felt something was missing.

"I found out I was not in my own act after a while," he said. Carlin ditched the wacky characters and started doing routines that reflected how he felt about life. The result disappointed many of his old fans. But the passion he poured into his new act gave him greater satisfaction and made him phenomenally successful.

Your passion might be whale watching or bird watching. It could be wine making or wine tasting. You get the idea. There is probably a group of fellow enthusiasts in your area. If not, start one.

Find your passion and then be passionate about it. Tell people about it. You can express yourself through a blog. You could express yourself through a Facebook page or Instagram or Pinterest pins. Perhaps your logo or business cards or business name could reflect your interest.

Here is an idea: Why not shoot a video related to your passionate interest? Show people how much you love that new boat, that favorite fishing hole, that home where George Washington once spent the night. Post your video on YouTube. Link it to your website and social media presence.

Join Facebook groups pertaining to your passion. Whatever it is, find your passion, and then go out and pursue it. You can tell everyone you meet, "I am a great Realtor®. I can help anybody get a great deal when they are buying or selling a home, but I am really passionate about homes_____ (put your specialty here)."

KEY TAKEAWAYS:

- Affinity marketing focuses on a community of individuals who share a passion or interest.

- Your own passion can open new markets for your services among like-minded people who respect your opinions.

- Almost any passion can enhance your real estate business, if you pursue it and make your interests known to others.

CHAPTER 10

Develop a Niche and Establish Yourself as the Best

When you market yourself with your niche it opens a world of opportunity that you would not normally have if you were just a generic agent. Some may feel like it is limiting your reach but it is quite the contrary.

Let me tell you a story about an agent who benefited from the niche strategy. This agent developed her niche and became the best at helping people buy or sell all the types of properties in her specific area of specialization. She was in a small market; she is not in a big, huge market. The average house price is around $200,000, and yet she is selling $30 million to $40 million a year consistently!

She sold $35 million in volume in 2012, when the housing market was just starting to recover from recession. That niche has really given her a great business. The interesting part is only half of the houses that she sells are in her small niche. She gets a lot of other business from people who are not buying or selling a house in her niche.

A niche is like rocket fuel for her real estate business. People who are buying a house or selling a house within her niche hire her because she is the expert in that niche. They put their house on the market with her, get to know her, realize she's an amazing Realtor®, and as a result, she meets a lot of people.

Those people can tell that she is great. She knows her market. She provides excellent customer service. She saves money for her buyers, makes more money for her sellers, and solves problems for both kinds of clients. Some of them go on to buy or sell properties that don't fit into her core business so she benefits when they give her their repeat business.

Other clients are quick to refer her to friends and relatives, who also might not fit within her niche. But all these people need a great Realtor®. The key is that she made vital connections with people while operating within her core area of specialization. She started out with nothing, and her niche has fueled the growth of the rest of her business.

Specializing in a particular niche does not mean you can not sell other properties. But building the core of your business by specializing in that niche gives you lots of power.

Everybody wants to work with an expert. Everybody wants to work with the best of the best at whatever they are doing. However, most Realtors® never bother to specialize. They assume the best strategy is to sell whatever they can whenever they can. It is simply not in the DNA of Realtors® to specialize in a niche. Consequently, they never become experts in any single area of specialization.

WHEN ONLY AN EXPERT WILL DO

Let's look at other industries. If you were arrested and you were facing the possibility of going to go to jail for 20 years, would you want to hire an attorney who is amazing at criminal cases and keeping clients out of jail, or would you prefer to hire a personal injury attorney who specializes in collecting money on lawsuits? Personally, I would prefer to work with the criminal attorney.

Who do you want to hire to help you if you need brain surgery? The answer is evident, you would hire a brain surgeon. But let me ask you a question. Would you hire an amazing dentist — the best dentist in the entire world, with accolades out the wazoo — to perform surgery on your brain? The answer is no, of course not.

The same thing applies in reverse. You would not hire that brain surgeon — even the best brain surgeon on earth — to do a root canal on your teeth. That is the reason you want to specialize. People want to work with an expert.

You can position yourself as an expert, grow your business in your niche, and then grow your business outside of your niche. Your expertise in a core area — your niche — will be your entryway to meeting an enormous number of people with properties to buy or sell within that niche.

You will quickly become an expert in your core area of focus, and it will be so much easier to get people to work with you. Let's say someone wants to buy a mountain property, and you are the local expert at mountain properties. Are they going to want to work with you or the agent who does a little bit of everything? Of course, the person interested in buying a mountain property will prefer to work with the mountain property expert.

AVOIDING "TYPECASTING"

One of the biggest concerns that most agents have: "I do not want to get stereotyped as only selling homes in that niche." I can understand your concern. A good actor does not want to be typecast, either. Actors hate to hear casting directors say, "Hey, you are only the funny actor. You are only the action movie actor. You are only the romantic movie actor." Once an actor gets typecast, it's very hard to get other roles.

Just as a good actor does not want to be typecast, neither do you. So, do not brand yourself as the niche. Do not say, "I'm the golf property agent." Instead, brand yourself as a great Realtor® who happens to know a lot about that niche. Do not be the golf property agent, be the agent who understands how to market homes on golf courses. "I do a great job on all the different properties out there, but I am also really, really good at helping you buy or sell a golf property."

In fact, you could put it in the beginning of every article or blog that you write. Remember the "Most Interesting Man in the World" ads for Dos Equis? His tagline was, "I do not always drink beer, but when I do, I drink Dos Equis." Let's say you want to start a blog about golf course properties. Every blog post might start out, "I do not only sell golf properties, but when I do, here is what I think about it." Let people know that you are good at all aspects of real estate, but you are especially good at selling properties in your niche.

3 STEPS TO BECOMING AN EXPERT

Here is the three-step process to becoming an expert in a specialty:

1. First, you need to identify your niche. I will tell you how to do that in just a minute.

2. Next, you have got to study the niche. You want to become the best of the best and genuinely know what you are talking about when it comes to buying or selling a house within your niche. You cannot fake it. You need to become amazing at helping people buy or sell a house inside your niche.

3. Then, you have to start marketing your expertise in that niche. "I am the best. I don't always sell golf properties, but when I do, I do it better than anyone. Here is why."

FINDING YOUR NICHE

How do you find your niche? Let's ask some questions. What are your strengths? What are things that you are good at or passionate about? Is there a real estate niche in which you have already sold a lot of houses? Maybe you have sold a lot of new construction, or you have sold a lot of vacant land, or you have sold a lot of multi-family investment property. Maybe you have sold a lot of houses in one general area of town or a specific neighborhood.

There are all sorts of niches on which you can focus. You can focus on waterfront, riverfront properties, intercoastal properties, lakefront properties, or homes within walking distance of a lake or beach. You can specialize in golf properties, historic houses, vacant land, country properties, homes on more than one acre, multi-family investment properties, mountain properties, downtown lofts, or homes with good views.

You could specialize in the properties within a specific ZIP code — especially exclusive or desirable ZIP codes. Some buyers would love an expert who could help them find a home — or an investment property — in the 90210 ZIP code of Beverly Hills, the 33109 of Miami Beach, Aspen's 81611, or the 94027 of Silicon Valley. Have you sold a ton of homes in an upscale or historic ZIP code in your area? That's a possible niche.

Here is another idea. Maybe you are a sensitive person who excels at showing empathy and talking to people about tough issues. It takes a special kind of person to do this. If that is you, consider targeting people who are getting a divorce or who are inheriting a house from a loved one. Often, those are emotional home sales, and your skills and caring attitude could really help buyers — or sellers — who are going through a rough time with their transactions.

Here is something important to remember. Do not stop at just one niche. You can have two, three, four, five niches, and once you get a niche up and running, start another one. I would focus on one niche at a time. Become the best of the best at golf course properties, for example, and then once you have achieved that, move on to new construction, or whatever it is. There are endless niches that you can make your own to grow your business.

STUDYING YOUR NICHE

I am going to use the golf course property example here. If you have decided you want to specialize in golf course properties. Start your research with Google. Google the phrase "Biggest mistakes to avoid when selling a golf course property." Google "Golf course properties," or, "Golf courses in my area," and just go through some of the different websites and get some ideas.

Find an expert in another marketplace or a professional golfer and ask them questions to find out more about the sport. If you already know how to play golf you have great information that others will not have. The details you can get from someone who does this in another market or from a professional golfer who does it for a living.

If you have never played golf but want to specialize in golf course properties, go out and play a few rounds. Look at the various homes for sale in golf course developments — not just from the street side, but from the golfer's point of view on the greens. Explore the neighborhood. Find out how the developers market the homes and which amenities are important to local golfers and homeowners.

Identify who is buying golf course homes in your area. That information will help you narrow down other interests and important aspects that you can use to market yourself.

Study the prices at which the homes were offered — as well as their actual selling prices. This information is available on your local MLS. The more information you can get on the things this customer likes and dislikes the better you will be able to market to them. All of this information will make you more of an expert on your chosen market.

MARKETING YOUR NICHE EXPERTISE

Once you reach the point at which you feel you are an expert, go out and start marketing yourself. Start up an Instagram page. Just start posting pictures; this is so easy. Go around with your phone, take 100, 200 pictures, and start posting them on your Instagram page: "John's golf course niche," or,

"Golf course expert," or whatever. Just start getting your interest and expertise out there for people to see.

Many of the suggestions from Chapter 8 will work here. Do YouTube videos where you talk about your niche. Going back to our golf niche example, give people a tour of the golf course neighborhood in your area. "Hey, here is a tour of such and such golf course neighborhood and why you would love to own a home here." Join groups. Start a blog. There are so many different ways that you can market yourself as the expert in your niche.

Just get out, look, research, and learn. That is how you can become an expert at a niche and use that niche to fuel your business.

KEY TAKEAWAYS:

- Developing expertise in a specific niche is an effective way to create a core business in real estate.

- Over time, identify yourself with additional specialties. Take measures not to "typecast" yourself.

- Developing niche business is a three-step process. Identify your niche, study it carefully, then market your expertise.

CHAPTER 11

Identify and Use Your Communication Strength

If you are a naturally amazing, talented speaker, spending all of your time writing or blogging to communicate with potential customers would be putting yourself at a disadvantage.

Equally, if you are an amazing writer, but the only way you have to communicate with prospects and clients is in person or on the phone. That would also be placing yourself at a big disadvantage.

Find your most powerful communication strength, then focus your marketing efforts in that area and get more business as a result. You can also find ways to minimize the communication styles that are least natural for you.

The more time you spend putting your communication strengths to work, the sooner you will reach your full potential. Do not waste time on unproductive communication types only to leave you feeling discouraged.

IDENTIFYING YOUR STRENGTHS

First, identify the way that you prefer to communicate. Think about the times you have communicated with people most effectively. Think about the times communication felt most natural or satisfying to you. Now, think about which of your communication efforts have received the most compliments from others.

Maybe you prefer public speaking, and you are an amazing public speaker. Perhaps you have given presentations and members of your audience have come up to you afterward and thanked you or praised your speech. If that is the case, learn how you can get public speaking engagements in your marketplace and grow your real estate business that way.

What about writing? If you are an amazing writer, find ways that you can write and grow your business. Perhaps you are not comfortable with public speaking or writing. Maybe your forte is talking to people one-on-one and building rapport. If that is you, there are other options that will let you focus on this strength.

START USING YOUR STRENGTH

Once you have identified your communication strength, then start using it more. If you are a writer, post. Create a Facebook page, if you have not done so already. Post on Facebook every day or start a blog. Blog about your favorite neighborhoods, their histories, their community events. Highlight some of their outstanding citizens. Celebrate their diversity, their architecture, their mature landscaping — whatever makes those neighborhoods great places to live. use your niche to talk about all of these things. Tie it all together this way.

To start blogging, purchase a domain name with a name that reflects your focus. Maybe include the name of your area, real estate blog, or your specialty in your domain name. You will also need a hosting service for your website. Then the type of message venue will be necessary.

One venue that is most popular is a basic WordPress blog. On your Facebook page, you could talk about your favorite neighborhoods, why you like them, and your new homes that come on the market. Start writing, and pretty soon you will begin to get search engine rankings. Business will be generated that way too.

Do not forget to post photographs and videos. If you have an Instagram or Pinterest page you can post your pictures there as well. You can connect your Instagram with Facebook and Only post one time and get them posted in both places. As you get more adept at communicating online, you can try targeting the different search engine words and use those to get business. There are lots of different ways to do this.

If speaking to groups and writing are not viable options for you, maybe your strength is that you are terrific at communicating one-on-one, and you are amazing at building a rapport with one individual at a time. In that case, you might want to try a method that puts you in a position to succeed.

If you have someone to develop leads for you — or even if you do not — you just might be happier trying some door knocking. Pick a neighborhood where you want to get listings and go door-to-door. Talk to the people in your community and get to know them. Ha ha ha! Who wants to door knock? But...if you do there is that option.

You could also attend local events, such as holiday celebrations, block parties, neighborhood barbecues, etc. Try volunteering for a community project or program. Even if there are a lot of people attending these events, you will find plenty of opportunities to chat with people individually and make contacts. Get out there and start meeting people, start building relationships, because those relationships are going to turn into more real estate business.

In addition, you will also make a lot of great friends. That is one of the reasons many agents love the real estate business. Making friends is a great way to generate business leads, but making friends is also a reward in itself.

You might be better in front of a crowd, try speaking at an engagement or hosting one your self. Instantly, a room full of people know of a great Realtor® — you — and if they are going to sell or buy a house, there is a good chance you are the first agent they will think of.

Make your presentation useful so it appeals to most people. Keep it basic so those who do not understand anything about real estate don't get lost in the words. Education is one of the best ways for people to learn who you are and what you do. Doing in a public event also gives you instant credibility.

One speech idea is to talk about what is happening in the marketplace. This will vary from time to time as local market conditions change, but your speech can rely on the same format time after time. Talk about the stats, talk about the trends, talk about what is hot, what is not.

You could talk about the advantages of buying an investment property compared to putting money in bonds or the stock market. Be willing to be controversial. If you are confident and passionate about real estate, get out there and tell people why it is a great investment.

If nothing else, people are going to talk about you. They are going to realize you believe in the value of real estate. Even if they do not agree with you, they are going to recognize that you are a great Realtor®, that you are very passionate about real estate, and that you can probably do a good job at helping them buy or sell a house.

WHAT TO AVOID

There are a couple of mistakes to avoid. You do not want your speech to be too "pitchy." Turning your speech into a transparent pitch for new business will only turn off your audience and guarantee that you are never invited back.

The goal of the speech should be to provide value and get people to know you as an expert in your marketplace. Devote 95 percent of your speech to providing valuable content. Then at the end, you can say, "You know what? If you want to contact me for any real estate questions, This is my contact information and website. I'll be happy to answer any of your questions about real estate."

Just add a one-minute elevator speech at the very end of your presentation to talk about why you are different from your competitors. Just tell them a little bit about what you do and why you are so good at it — you specialize in the local market or in certain kinds of homes found in the neighborhood. This might be a great place to insert your niche, as we discussed in Chapter 9.

Keep it short and then move along. Remember, you are not here to wham 'em over the head and close an immediate sale. Just show them, through your presentation, that you are knowledgeable, likable, approachable, and that they would benefit by working with you.

Once you develop a speech about real estate, you can start doing free speeches all over town. Most organizations need good speakers. There is more demand for good speakers than there are speakers available. Instead of having a conversation with one individual you meet at the grocery store, you can give your stock speech to 100, 200, 500 people, or more, and get better known by all the people in your marketplace.

Think of it this way: each speech to an audience of 50 is roughly equal to one or two listing appointments.

KEY TAKEAWAYS:

- Identify the method of communication you prefer and that works best for you.

- Once you've identified your communication strength, use it to full advantage. For example:

If you excel at public speaking, join civic organizations, volunteer to be a guest speaker, or host events at which you speak.

If you are a good writer, use Facebook, Instagram, blogging, and other ways to reach people.

If you are best at one-on-one communication, try cold calling, door knocking, or interactions at local events and volunteer opportunities.

- Create and practice your elevator speech — a sentence or two about how you're better than your competition and why people should work with you.

CHAPTER 12

Build Your Clientele

Another way you can gain an advantage over your competition and grow your real estate business is to build up your clientele. Obviously, getting to know more people and building your clientele will increase your business. This is how successful agents have a never ending flow of clients. This is a process and is not something that happens overnight but with the right processes and followup can happen relatively quickly.

Wouldn't it be nice if you came into the office and you just knew that no matter what, every single day, every single month, a certain amount of new business would come through your door?

You can do that when you build up a loyal clientele — people who worked with you in the past. People who give you their repeat business and who also refer new business to you. Here is an example of how this really works.

I will tell you a little story about a guy who used this advantage in his business. This man's name is Joe

Girard. He is not a real estate salesman. Joe Girard is a car salesman.

But Joe had a great system for building his clientele. As a result, according to the *Guinness Book of World Records,* he was the world's greatest salesman. Rather than just saying, "I'm the best. I'm number one," he actually had the *Guinness Book of World Records* do research, and they determined that Joe Girard had sold more vehicles than any other individual. According to their criteria, Joe Girard was the *world's greatest salesperson.*

When he was relatively new in the car sales business, he was struggling a bit. He was paying his bills, doing OK, but he wanted to grow his business. When he took the job at the dealership, he had promised the owner, "I won't get my sales from people who walk in the door. I will bring my sales in on my own efforts." As a result, he struggled to get enough business because he did not benefit from any of the walk-in traffic that dealership had.

One day, Joe went to a funeral. It was a Catholic funeral, and he saw that a lot of mass cards were being given out to the attendees. In fact, there were enough mass cards for everybody at the funeral.

Curious, he went and talked to the funeral director and asked, "Hey, how in the world do you know how many mass cards to print? 'Cause if you print too many, you've got to throw them away. If you don't print enough, not everybody's going to have one."

The funeral director said, "You know what? Most funerals, it always comes out to about 250 cards that I need to print. So, I get 250 printed up for every funeral, and we almost never run out, and we hardly have to throw any away because, usually, about 250 people show up at any type of funeral."

Weeks later, Joe went to another funeral and asked the funeral director the same question. The funeral director gave the same answer: "Oh, we print about 250. That's how many cards we have in order to make sure that everybody gets a card, and we don't have to throw that many away."

Then Joe went to a wedding and asked the minister about attendance. The minister said. "We have about 500 people show up at most weddings. We've got 250 on the bride's side and 250 on the groom's side."

As a result of his experiences at the funerals and wedding, Joe recognized a pattern, which he began to call his Law of 250. In a nutshell, the law states that most people know about 250 people who care about them enough to go to a funeral when they pass away or to go to a wedding when they get married. Yes, there probably are some instances where people know more people or fewer people, but in general, about 250 people care about somebody enough to go to their funeral or go to their wedding.

So, Joe went home and realized, "If I can do a great job for a customer, not only am I going to gain that customer's possible repeat business down the road. I'm also going to gain 250 additional, potential customers who care enough about that person that they may ask for their opinion or ask for their referral for buying a car." Joe then put together a great system that enabled him consistently to stay in touch with all of his past clients. Each of those clients represented approximately 250 possible referrals.

So, that is what you can do. Figure out a way to stay in touch with all of your past customers — in fact, your entire sphere of influence. By continuing your communication with past customers, you change the nature of your marketing from a one-time *transactional* model to an ongoing *relationship-based* model. At the same time, you grow a clientele that achieves a critical mass — enough repeat business and referrals to ensure sustained growth. These are the customers you can expect to just walk through your door.

HOW JOE DID IT

Here is what Joe Girard did to cultivate all of his past customers. He knew if he just sold them a car and they never heard from him again, he probably would not gain their repeat and referral business. So, every month, he would mail out a little postcard or a handwritten note that said, "I like you." That is all it was; it just said, "I'm Joe Girard. I like you." Every single month, he would mail it out to past customers and make sure they did not forget about Joe Girard.

Obviously, he also provided great service. There is a lot more to what he did, but the bottom line is he did a good job for his customers and worked hard, just like you work hard for your customers. The difference was that he stayed in touch, so they would send him referrals and never forget him.

You can do the same thing. You could start up an email newsletter. You could mail postcards. With today's electronic innovations and capabilities, you can automate your process, so that it happens regularly, consistently, and with minimal effort. Whatever method you choose, if you stay in touch with each of your customers and take great care of them, you can build up an amazing clientele that will feed you and pay your bills for the rest of your life.

KEY TAKEAWAYS:

- Keep building your clientele. First-time clients form the basis for repeat business and referrals.

- Joe Girard's Law of 250 states that on average, every individual exerts influence over approximately 250 others.

- Keeping in touch with every past customer keeps them aware of you. It also converts a transactional interaction to an ongoing personal relationship.

- Newsletters and emails are two examples of ways customer contacts can be automated.

CHAPTER 13

New at the Game? Step Up to Bat!

If you are just getting started in the real estate business, here are some tips that will make the transition easier. The first thing I would recommend is taking maximum advantage of your brokerage's training programs. A lot of companies have great training programs that can really help you get started and get going fast.

Whatever training programs are available to you, tap into them. Take the time to sit down, watch the training videos, read the books, whatever it is. Take the time to learn and study so you can become the best.

When you are starting out as an agent, it can be challenging to get business. People who want to buy or sell homes might be hesitant to work with you. If you have not established a reputation yet, use your brokerage's credibility to help you get customers.

Consider teaming up with an experienced agent or rely on your broker for advice. Ask them questions and have them guide you through your first couple of deals. It can be intimidating trying to help your first customer all by yourself.

Do not be afraid to ask someone at your brokerage to look over your shoulder, making sure you have got everything figured out. Even the most successful Realtors® started somewhere, and most would probably say they benefited from the experience and guidance of at least one mentor.

When you are starting out, it's helpful to have some money saved up. Sometimes it can take 60 to 90 days to start receiving commissions for closings. That is the unfortunate reality of real estate and other commission-based occupations.

SEASONAL FACTORS AFFECT SALES

Real estate prices can fluctuate because of seasonal changes, especially the school year or holiday seasons. Typically, many home buyers and sellers would rather wait to move during the summer. June is especially busy, and July 31st is the busiest moving day of the year.

Waiting for summer is less disruptive for school-age children. They have more free time to pack and help move. They also get more time to acclimate to a new neighborhood and school district before school resumes in the fall.

Seasonal patterns vary by region, but in general, weather can affect the supply and demand of housing.

People also prefer not to move during the holiday season, from November to January. Investopedia cites reasons such as family obligations, year-end deadlines, inclement weather, and the financial strain holidays place on family budgets.

If you're dedicated to understanding your local real estate market, you'll track the important market metrics for your area every month. You'll be able to identify shifts in listing prices and to calculate average sales prices.

That will give you advance knowledge of trends that could affect your clients and your business. Your knowledge will allow you to approach home buyers and advise them on the best times to make lower-than-listed purchases.

Disclaimer, as this book is being published the market is at a momentum not seen for many years and expected to continue for at least one more year. Everything that was mentioned above is irrelevant at this time. My recommendation is to get it while you can.

HOW'S YOUR FINANCIAL PLAN?

You have probably noticed how I keep referring to your real estate career as a "business." As a real estate agent, the IRS and your state will almost certainly treat you as a business owner for tax purposes.

Unfortunately, one real estate industry expert estimates that more than 80 percent of real estate agents have no financial plan. The slow months are the perfect time to review your finances and create a plan but the better time to do it is before you get started. Here are some questions you should ask yourself:

- How much did I spend last year?

- What did I spend my money on?

- Did I take advantage of every available tax write-off for my business?

- Did I waste money on tools that I did not use or that were unproductive?
- What should next year's annual budget be?

- Should I incorporate my business and pay myself a salary?

- Do I need to be paying quarterly taxes?

- How can I save more?

- Could my business invest to make more money?

Spend some time doing the necessary research and consulting experts to make sure you answer each of these important questions.

Many agents, just starting out, work a second job if necessary to cover the bills and routine expenses while building their real estate business. If you do not have some else in your household that can make the ends meet you may consider this. If you do work another job, you might want to share your real estate ambitions with your coworkers at the second job. Each of those coworkers is a potential customer or referral for the future. If you impress them with your hard work, knowledge, and trustworthiness, perhaps they will go to you for their future needs when buying or selling a home.

Above all, remember, if you try hard and stay committed, you'll make it. I guarantee it! Sometimes it will take a little bit more work, but once you get going, real estate is an extremely rewarding career. If you are willing to work harder than you have ever worked in your life for six months to a year, you can get your business started, and you are going to love it.

BUILD YOUR BOOK OF BUSINESS

When starting out, you will want to do anything you can to bring in new customers. A lot of agents struggle with the fact that they are competing with other agents who are more experienced. Just start where you are and give a large clientele time to develop naturally.

All you need is one or two customers who will put their trust in you and say, "You know what? I'm willing to work with you to help me buy or sell my house." You just need to convince one person to take a chance, and that will lead to credibility, experience, and confidence that you know what you are doing, and you can help them.

MAKE BEING NEW AN ADVANTAGE

One of your biggest challenges as a new real estate agent is overcoming the belief that "No one will work with me because I am new."

When you are talking to prospective clients — or anyone else, really — about your real estate business, do not position yourself as being new and not knowing what you are doing. Position yourself with excitement to start this new journey, show your enthusiasm, share the things you DO know and you will see the confidence begin to rise within you. That confidence will get you the business that you want.

Here is a fact: innovation comes from new companies and new Realtors®. You may be way more innovative than the Realtor® who has already been in the business for 30 years and does not want to try anything new. That realization should provide you with confidence and plenty of motivation.

Remember what I said about Hewlett-Packard in Chapter 4? Do you think that Hewlett-Packard would have created the iPhone? Even though they had been in business decades at the time, it took an upstart company like Apple to create the iPhone.

Unfortunately for Hewlett-Packard, they are no longer an innovative computer company. They are creating a lot of printers and a few computers, but they are not changing lives or fulfilling dreams with the newest, cutting-edge technology.

In the same way, a new agent like you, just starting out, may have a lot more cutting-edge, innovative ideas that can help your customers. It is valuable to look at real estate through a fresh set of eyes, without the "but we have always done it that way!" attitude that many people who have been in the business for 20 or 30 years might have.

START WITH PEOPLE YOU KNOW

So, if you are intent on building your real estate book of business from scratch, where should you start? A great place to find your customers is to start is with your friends, your neighbors, your family, former coworkers, people you grew up with, former teachers — really, anyone you know.

Reach out to anyone you know in your area and just let them know, "Hey, I went into real estate, and I'd be excited to help you with any of your real estate needs. Who do you know that is looking to buy or sell a property this year?"

Do not be offended if they say they do not know. Some people may hire you, some people may not. That is not the end of the world. The point is to get out there, let people know you are in the real estate business, and start building your reputation as an agent who is enthusiastic and willing to work hard.

When anybody decides to work with you, be appreciative and thankful you get their business. If somebody turns you down because you are new, stay in touch with them. Maybe when you get your business up and running and you have proved yourself as a successful Realtor®, they will try you out on a future transaction.

Even people who do not hire you can be valuable sources of referrals. Maybe they have a friend or neighbor who wants to sell a house or who is ready to buy one. Think back on Joe Girard's Law of 250 from Chapter 11. Treating people well and building relationships is like dropping a pebble in a pond. The ripples spread out wider and wider. Eventually, the relationships you build will bring reliable business to your door.

BENEFITS OF WORKING WITH BUYERS

Be willing to work with buyers. It might sound silly, but many real estate agents do not want to work with them. Many agents find buyers can be challenging and frustrating to work with. The perception is that buyers are more labor-intensive. The agent might have to travel around to show them multiple houses, and if they are not clear about what they want — or they are just plain indecisive — it can be difficult.

But it is so much easier to get buyers to put their confidence in you than it is to get sellers to list their house with you.

Think of it this way: you are getting paid to learn the real estate marketplace. Working with buyers, you will learn the neighborhoods. You will learn the market. You will learn what's hot. You will learn how much homes sell for and what makes some more desirable than others. You will be compensated for your training as soon as you sell a house to a buyer.

THRIVING IN ALL SEASONs

Whether you are in a busy season or a slow season, the most important thing to remember is you have control over it.

I was told a story once that really stuck with me. In the early 1920's there were two general store owners. Each store owner was across the street from the other. One of the store owners watch each day as the other store owner had people entering and exiting his store all day while he had only a few. One day he decided to cross the street and ask the other store owner what he was doing it. He asked the other store owner, "How do manage to keep customers coming into your store all day, every day in such a deep depression?" The other store owner replied,"What depression?"

My point is you do not have to slow down just because the market does. All you do is keep doing what you do every day and the business will keep coming the way it does every day. What you focus on will actually improve.

PRIMING THE PUMP

An important tip that I would recommend is to have a little bit of patience. Sometimes it takes time to get your business moving. I will give you a little parable about how this works. Have you ever seen an old well pump? I am talking about an old-fashioned hand pump where you pump water from a well that is deep in the ground.

Most people pump the handle a few times but do not get any water. They do not realize this, but they have to prime the pump. The pump must have water slowly come up the pipe until it reaches the top. You may have to pump it many and multiple times before you get any water. Once the water begins to flow there will be a continual stream and the force to keep it flowing will be minor in comparison to the force it took to prime it.

Anything that you decide to start will require the same effort. You may have to talk to many different leads. People may tell you they are looking in a few months. If you give up too fast you will be missing out on a waterfall of business that is coming.

But if you are consistently priming the pump, the business will begin to flow and the effort will be minimal.

FOCUS, FOCUS, FOCUS!

Sharpen your focus. Do not try to chase too many goals at once. Maybe you have heard the Chinese saying, "He who chases two rabbits catches none." I would recommend focusing on one thing at a time, one goal, one business strategy, rather than trying to focus on multiple strategies.

Life is a marathon, not a sprint. If you are going to be successful in real estate for 5, 10, 20, or 30 years, you are going to have plenty of time to try out all different ideas. But in the beginning, you are going to get better results by channeling all of your energy into one idea, one marketing strategy, or one real estate niche. Focusing all your energy on one opportunity will take you way further than trying to chase several "rabbits."

CULTIVATE THE TRAITS OF A WINNER

Winners in the game of real estate — or the game of life — almost always exhibit certain characteristics. Learn to adopt those characteristics, and you can be a winner too. Here are the traits you should work to cultivate:

Confidence: If you are not naturally confident, then go back into the earlier chapters and put together an amazing plan. When you have a rock-solid plan, you cannot help but be confident in your abilities to help that customer.

Hard Work: Real estate is a tremendously rewarding career, but it is going to take time and energy to get your career going. That might entail doing more research on your local market. It might mean putting in more hours or working weekends to serve your customers. Whatever effort you have to put in will be rewarded.

Being a People Person: Learn how to get along with people. In Chapter 3, I detailed the process of making friends with people. These are skills that can be learned, practiced, and perfected, even if you are normally shy or a loner. With effort, you can learn to listen to people, to show genuine care for their concerns, and to put yourself in a position to help them meet their needs and goals.

Becoming Tech-Savvy: In addition, you want to learn some of the technology that is required. You do not have to be a techie, but you want to be able to use the basic technology to help your customers reach their goals. If an iPad will help you pull up listings while you are showing buyers houses out in the field, then get an iPad and learn how to use it. Understanding social media will open up new ways to share your business messaging with prospects and clients. Automating your follow-up contacts with past customers will help build warm relationships, while expending less time and effort.

Eagerness to Listen and Learn: Here is a final trait worth cultivating if you want to be a winner in the real estate game. Be eager to listen and eager to learn. Listen to your customers. Listen to your coworkers and mentors. You have two ears and one mouth for a reason — to listen twice as much as you speak! People want to work with someone who will listen to them.

The more you open yourself to listening, the quicker you will learn how to build your business, meet your customers' needs and goals, and achieve success in your business. That can be one of your competitive advantages in real estate: "I listen, and I help you reach your goals. I take your thoughts and your input into consideration."

I will make you a promise. Be patient and stay optimistic. Immerse yourself in real estate, take advantage of every opportunity, whether your prospect is selling a home or wants to buy one. Practice developing the traits of a winner and work hard for every one of your customers. Do all this, and you will have amazing success in real estate.

KEY TAKEAWAYS:

- If you are a new agent, prepare for the time it may take to develop your business. Have savings in place and consider taking a part-time job.

- Take advantage of any training and guidance your brokerage offers. Rely on your broker's credibility while building your own with clients.

- If you are new to the real estate business, turn that into an advantage. New agents are often more innovative and energetic than their veteran counterparts.

- Cultivate the traits of a winner: confidence, hard work, people skills, technical understanding, eagerness to listen and learn

- While building your book of business, be willing to work with buyers. The extra work you do in learning your market and building relationships will pay off in the long run.

Joining a Team that makes a Difference in Your Future

There are many options available to agents and not all of them choose to be part of the same team...that is why there are options! All joking aside, I joined my current brokerage in 2016 because of all the reasons I talked about in this book.

We offer over 50 training sessions a week that you can take part in. These trainings are on everything you can imagine from beginning your real estate career, making it rain customers, your financial future, laws, contracts and so much more.

You have a very real opportunity to earn 100% of your commissions and you never have to pay a desk fee or franchise fees, marketing costs, or anything. There is a small technology fee that is less than one fifth of the cost of only one of the CRM programs available to you as an agent.

If you ever wanted to own a part of a world wide successful company, we give you that opportunity with stock options. At the time of this writing I have a real investment into this fantastic forward looking company that is paying big for me.

Building your career with me by your side has it's advantages too. I grew up in real estate and have managed sales teams for more than 25 years. I am a serial entrepreneur, owning several businesses, I have learned what it takes to be your own boss. I have certifications with Ziglar Legacy, Robbins-Madanes Coaching and believe in continual education as a tool to set yourself apart from the rest. At this time I am enrolled in a doctorate program for natural medicine.

Additionally, at no cost to the agent, we offer a chance to earn passive income from the efforts of those who join at your recommendation. There are many agents, as well as myself, that dedicate themselves to helping their agents to learn the success of this program and the secret of success real estate and are now making incomes that will take care of them even when they retire.

The progress of this company is never ending. We've partnered with successful businesses and business people who are dedicated to the success of our company, and continue to look for solutions to add more value to you and your clients.

We even took it another step and now offer group health insurance at real group discounts.

We offer mentorships to new agents coming onboard to help with the transition and to help with questions and motivation.

There is a very cool online platform where we all participate and join in the training and meetings, all from the cloud.

Apart from all of these things, you want someone on your side to help and support you. Someone one who has been through the fire and came out shining like a diamond.

The next step is to take action. This is the single most important step to reaching your goals. You can dream all you want, plan until you cannot think of another detail but if you do not take action, nothing will happen. Take action on your future today. Give me a call or email.

Best Regards,

Janna Valencia
janna@jannavalencia.com
210-850-7568

www.ingramcontent.com/pod-product-compliance
Lightning Source LLC
Chambersburg PA
CBHW062019200326
41519CB00017B/4846